Table of Contents

What Is Good Writing? 2

    Be Specific 3

    Show, Don't Tell 4

    Focus 5

    Trim the Fat 7

    Be Original 8

How to Write Your Paper — Eight Easy Steps 9

Step 1. Pick A Good Topic 10

Step 2. Write your Thesis 11

Step 3. Make a Detailed Outline 12

Step 4. How to Write Part I — Your Introduction 14

    Begin With a Story 15

    Begin With a Bold Statement 16

    Begin With a Question 16

    Begin With a Quotation 17

    Begin With a Paradox 17

Step 5 How to Write Part II — Your Argument 19

    Logical Proof 20

    Emotional Proof 23

Step 6. How to Write Part III — Prove Your Opponents Wrong 24

Step 7. How to Write Part IV — Your Conclusion 25

Step 8. Revise and Edit Your Paper 28

Your Finished Paper 31

S+T+R+O+N+G® Study Skills Program   © Silbert & Bress Publications

What Is Good Writing?

What Is good writing? Tough question. Unlike math or science, writing has no set answers, no true or false, no formulas.

To make matters worse, English teachers have their own ideas about what good writing is, and not all of them agree! Some worry mostly about grammar. Others want to see how well you can express yourself in original, or creative, ways. Some want you to follow the five-paragraph formula, while others want you to write more freely.

This can get very frustrating. And just in case you're thinking that you don't have to learn how to write well, that whatever you do for the rest of your life, it sure won't involve writing, guess what? In the real world, *everyone* has to write! For example, if you go to college, you'll probably take many courses that require writing papers such as English, History or Psychology. When you enter the job market, you'll almost certainly have to write your ideas and develop them well. You see, communicating ideas clearly and developing a good argument (to sell yourself and your ideas), is often the ticket to higher pay and promotions.

The good news is, almost every English teacher agrees on certain keys to good writing. If you take these suggestions and use them in your writing, you'll be instantly a better writer.

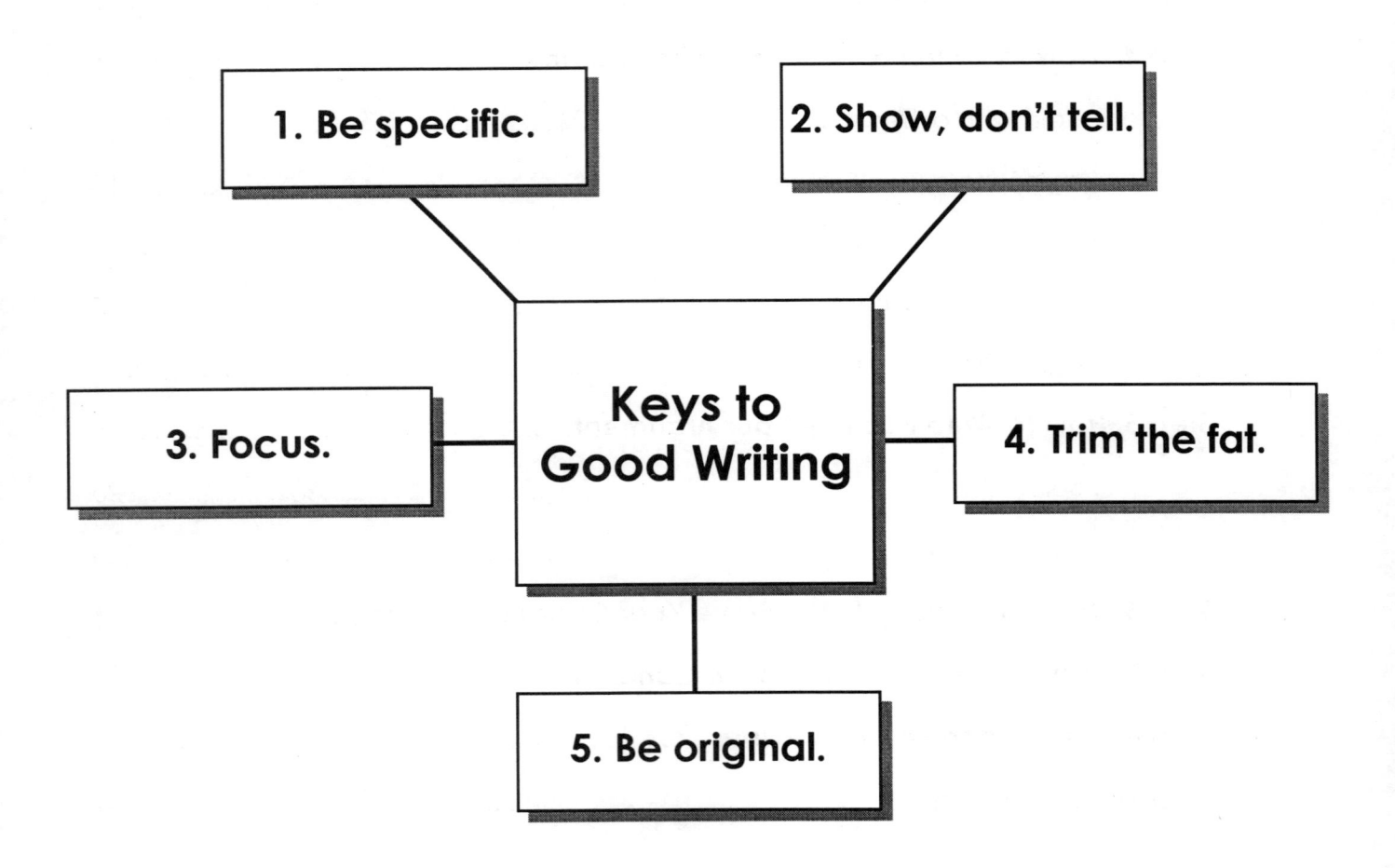

Keys to Good Writing

1. Be specific.
2. Show, don't tell.
3. Focus.
4. Trim the fat.
5. Be original.

Let's take these one at a time.

1. Be specific.

Here's the situation: you have a paper to write, and your teacher tells you it has to be at least three pages long. You start writing, and you only have two pages worth of writing. What do you do?

Well, if you're like most students, you just tack a couple of paragraphs onto the end, and ta-da! Three pages.

There's only one problem: your teacher can tell you've done this, because the last two paragraphs stink! They are repetitive, too general, or just plain boring. So you've made it three pages long, but it gets a lousy grade anyway. And you've done nothing to improve your writing skills, so you haven't learned a thing.

What you might not know is that the way to make your papers longer is not to add, but to *specify*. In other words, **be specific!** If you use more examples, quotations, and details, your paper will be longer, *and* it will be better.

Next time you get a paper assignment and complain that you have to write too much, ask yourself this question: how do people write *books*? How, for example, can a book about prayer flags in Tibet be 300 pages long?

The answer is that it is detailed. Good writers use many examples and details.

You can do the same thing.

Here's a sample paragraph from a high-school paper:

```
Every time I try to be self-reliant, I get knocked down. I have to
worry about my parents, my friends, and my teachers. I can never do
what I want to do.
```

Now here's the same paragraph with some detail added.

```
Every time I try to be self-reliant, I get knocked down. I have to
worry about my parents, my friends, and my teachers. When I wanted to
be in the jazz band, my parents told me that I needed to concentrate on
studying, my friends told me I was a nerd, and my math teacher got mad
because he wanted me to try out for football instead. I can never do
what I want to do.
```

2. Show, don't tell.

What we just showed you is something that we all know: when we communicate with our friends, with our family members, or with our teachers, the only way they really understand what we are trying to tell them is if we *show* them what we mean.

If you tell your friend that John is a jerk, then your friend will probably say something like, "Why? What did he do?" So you tell a story about what John did the night before, how he yelled at his girlfriend during an argument. Then your friend will nod in agreement. "Wow, he *is* a jerk!" she might say.

Like everyone, your friend needs to be *shown*, not told. When people tell you what you should think, don't you just hate it? So don't make the same mistake when you write. From now on, **show, don't tell.**

Too often you might write a sentence like, "I think capital punishment is wrong because innocent people may be put to death," and then move on to your next reason why you think it's wrong. But nobody will be convinced by this. After you write such a sentence, then you need to *show* what you mean. Write about a particular person who was wrongly killed: if you name his name, mention his family, discuss what prison was like for him, then your reader will begin to agree with you.

See, the idea is to get *your reader* to say, "Oh, I see. Capital punishment *is* wrong," instead of writing it over and over yourself. And the way to do that is by *showing*.

So, when you are making a point in your paper, don't just say it and move on. Say it, then show it. Illustrate the point you're making by using an example, or by telling a story, or by quoting the story you are writing about.

When you are making a point, don't just say it. Say it, then show it.

🖎 **Now you try it:** Write a sentence about one of the topics listed below. Then show what you mean by illustrating your point with an example:

- The value of sports in school
- Underage drinking
- The value of religion

- My connection with nature
- The best kind of music
- TV: good or bad?

_____
_____
_____
_____

Improve Your Writing Skills

3. Focus.

When you get your paper back, chances are your teacher has commented on your paper's *focus*. "You need to narrow your focus," your teacher might have written. Or, "The paper loses its focus." Or, "This essay isn't focused at all."

Almost all good writing, whether it's a short story by Alice Walker, an environmental essay by Peter Matthiessen, or an article in *Sports Illustrated* about college athletics, is *focused*. It leaves out information that has nothing to do with the topic. Like you, the writer is a smart person with much to say, and he or she also has to be on guard to keep unnecessary information out of the writing.

First, ***narrow your focus:*** You might think that if you keep the topic of your paper general enough, then you will have more to say, so you will get a better grade. Nope. Instead, the more *specific* your topic is, the more focused your paper will be, and the more likely it will be that you get a good grade.

If your paper is very general in the beginning, then it probably won't be focused at any point in the paper. So, narrow your focus right from the start. If you're writing a research paper on the environment, for example, don't focus on the environment in general. That's too broad. Instead, focus on some aspect of the environment.

Here's how you might narrow your focus:

The environment

⬇ ⬇ ⬇

Harm we have done to the environment

⬇ ⬇

The ozone layer

⬇

What's wrong with the ozone layer, and what can be done about it

So, a paper that might have had as its focus, "What can be done to improve the environment"—a paper that might mention recycling in one paragraph and the ozone layer in the next, and therefore would not be well focused—is now about one specific topic: the hole in the ozone layer, and what's being done to fix it. In fact, we can narrow that topic even further, by focusing on what the government has done about it, or companies that have adjusted their policies to lower the amount of pollutants they put into the atmosphere. We might end up with a really specific focus, like how Australians are getting skin cancer at a terrible rate because of the hole in the ozone layer.

Then, **keep your focus.** After you have narrowed your focus, you have to stay focused. This means sticking to your topic, and not putting in tons of information that is not about your topic.

Again, here's the key: have a specific thesis to begin with. Then you won't lose focus. When teachers write comments about your paper not being focused enough, they can show you exactly which paragraphs lose focus. But the probable source of the problem is that you weren't focused enough to begin with.

Once you get focused, stay focused.

How do you stay focused?

a. **Make an outline.**
   If you know where you're going, you won't wander down side streets. So give yourself directions, then follow them. Outline your paper. And for every step of your outline, try to use some specific examples to prove your point.

b. **Use transitions.**
   Transitional words, phrases or sentences keep your paper unified. They're very important. If you force yourself to begin almost every paragraph with a transition, then your paper will almost certainly stay focused.

Here are some good transitional words and phrases:

- **To add a point:** furthermore, besides, finally, in addition to, moreover, also
- **To emphasize:** above all, indeed, in fact, in other words, most important
- **To show cause and effect:** as a result, consequently, therefore, thus, hence
- **To use an example:** for example, for instance
- **To show progression:** first, second, third, furthermore
- **To show contrast:** but, however, in contrast, instead, nevertheless, on the contrary, on the other hand, still, unfortunately, rather, at least
- **To conclude:** therefore, to sum up, in brief, in general, for these reasons, finally, in conclusion

---

When you hear people say that a paper "flows" or that its ideas don't "flow," what people are really talking about are transitions. Are there transitions from one idea to the next? Are you connecting all your ideas?

4. Trim the fat.

What we've been talking about is how to write more efficiently—how to focus your ideas and not stray from your thesis. But you can also improve your writing by **"trimming the fat"**—cutting out excessive words, and replacing general words with active, accurate words.

Too many students think that the way to write is to be safe, to say "I think" or "In my opinion," or "I feel". But this has the opposite effect you think it does. Instead of strengthening your statement, it weakens it. Look at the difference "trimming the fat" makes:

"...that trashes half my paper—who do they think I am, Shakespeare?"

```
- I personally feel that capital punishment should be abolished.
- Capital punishment should be abolished.
```

The first one is weak because it makes you think, "Well, that's just your opinion." The second one is strong because it just states your opinion without being wishy-washy about it.

Here's an example of a paragraph that contains excess words and weak, general verbs:

```
    In my opinion, if the government of the United States doesn't make
all these companies do a much better job of cutting out the things that
make the ozone layer worse, then things are going to get really bad in
a very short time.
```

Try not to use the following words:
things, really, very, personally, I feel.
They rarely add anything to your paper.

Now here's that same sentence, with excess words taken out, and with stronger, more specific words to replace weak words like "things," "really" and "very." Again, look at the difference "trimming the fat" makes!

```
    If the government doesn't force companies to do their part to ensure
that the ozone layer isn't further depleted, then the atmosphere will
continue to deteriorate quickly.
```

5. Be Original.

What will make your paper stand out from the rest? You!

Your "voice," your personality, your style, your opinions. But first, you need to change how you see yourself.

You are probably not used to seeing yourself as a writer, as a smart person with something to say—someone whose opinion counts. But you are! You have your own perspective on things that are happening around you, your own opinion. Don't keep your interesting self out of your papers, **be original!**

Most students are so afraid of writing poorly that their fear *makes* them write poorly! They end up writing cautiously, taking the safe path, using safe words, writing short paragraphs. The result: BOOORING!

You wouldn't like reading such a paper if it were in your favorite magazine, would you? Of course not. You probably like to read articles that grab your attention, that are written in an interesting way, by a writer who's not afraid to use his or her "voice," opinion, or experiences.

You need to see yourself as the same kind of writer, one who will write interesting papers, not boring, safe papers.

So don't play it safe all the time. Write interesting introductions (see page 15), use original language to describe ordinary events, and don't be afraid to include your own opinion (unless your teacher tells you not to).

You need to see yourself as a smart person who can write original, not boring, papers.

"...you want ORIGINAL, I'll give you ORIGINAL! Once upon a time..."

Improve Your Writing Skills

Writing Your Paper—in 8 Easy Steps

In almost all the writing you do, whether in school or out, you are trying to persuade someone about something—to make an argument, in other words. Whether you are writing an essay about Shakespeare's *Hamlet*, a paper on capital punishment, or an e-mail letter to your friend, you are usually trying to convince your reader of something—that Hamlet's main problem is that he thinks too much, that capital punishment does nothing to deter crime, or that *The Empire Strikes Back* is better than *Star Wars*.

We're sure that you'll want to be as convincing as possible, so in the following pages we'll show you how to organize your paper so that it will be convincing to the max. We'll do this by showing you how to move from a **description** of your issue to your recommendation on what to **do** about your issue.

Here are the 8 easy steps; in the following pages we'll walk you through them one at at time. Just answer some questions and add some details, and soon you'll have **YOUR PAPER!**

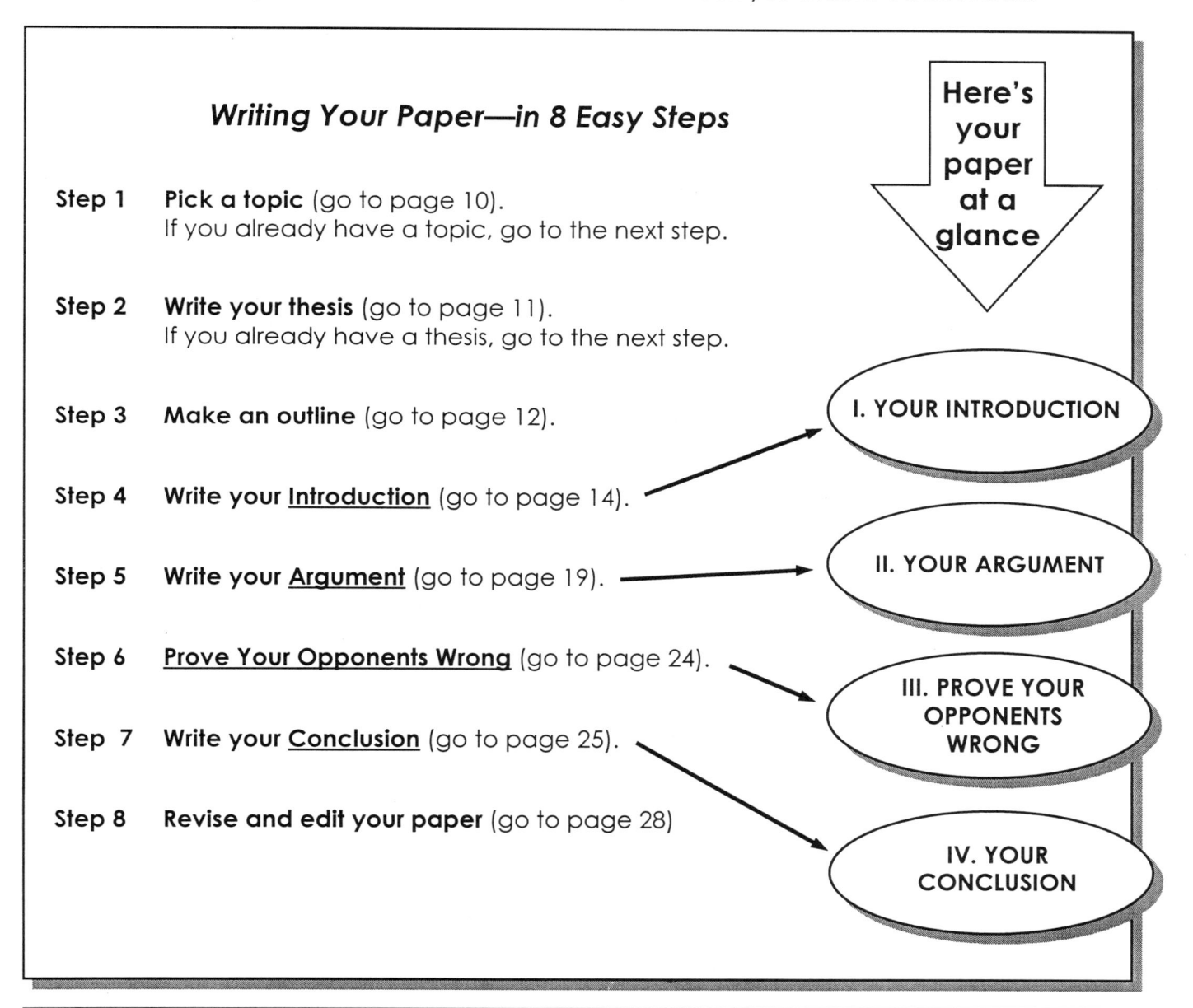

Writing Your Paper—in 8 Easy Steps

Here's your paper at a glance ⬇

- **Step 1** **Pick a topic** (go to page 10).
  If you already have a topic, go to the next step.

- **Step 2** **Write your thesis** (go to page 11).
  If you already have a thesis, go to the next step.

- **Step 3** **Make an outline** (go to page 12).

- **Step 4** **Write your Introduction** (go to page 14). → **I. YOUR INTRODUCTION**

- **Step 5** **Write your Argument** (go to page 19). → **II. YOUR ARGUMENT**

- **Step 6** **Prove Your Opponents Wrong** (go to page 24). → **III. PROVE YOUR OPPONENTS WRONG**

- **Step 7** **Write your Conclusion** (go to page 25).

- **Step 8** **Revise and edit your paper** (go to page 28) → **IV. YOUR CONCLUSION**

Step 1. Pick A Good Topic

Step 1. Pick A Good Topic

If you can pick your own topic for a paper, that's great. Pick something that interests you, not something you think you *should* write about. Instead of writing about a general or typical topic like abortion or capital punishment, write about something you are interested in, whether it's hiking or car engines.

In most classes, however, the teacher will ask you to write about a particular topic, or give you some to choose from. With that in mind, we'll use as examples two papers on topics from a list given to a high school class: the *environment* (the ozone-layer paper we mentioned earlier) and *education*.

As you go through this workbook, we'd like you to practice what we tell you about by writing a rough draft of a paper in the space we've provided or on your computer word processor. By the end of this book you will have written a good persuasive paper!

So please pick a topic (feel free to select from the list below), and every time we ask you to try something (after we say, *Now You Try It*), write on that same topic.

- the value of sports in school
- underage drinking
- the value of religion
- my connection with nature
- the best kind of music
- TV: good or bad?

Now You Try It: In the space below or on a computer word processor, write down some ideas you have about the topic you picked. Just scribble down some thoughts you have about the topic, what you might say about it in this paper, some examples you might use. Don't stop to think. (This is called *freewriting*.)

_____

_____

_____

_____

_____

_____

_____

_____

_____

_____

Step 2. Write Your Thesis

Step 2. Write Your Thesis

Write a **clear, specific thesis**. What we call your thesis can be many things, but usually it's what you are going to prove in your paper. Sometimes, if your paper isn't trying to prove anything, but just trying to show the reader something, it's not so much a thesis as it is a focus. So, what is your thesis, for the paper we're asking you to write? What is your focus?

Before you begin writing your paper, you should write down a sentence or two explaining exactly what you intend to say. This may not be exactly how you write it in your paper. For now, it's a guide, to give you some direction. Make it *clear, assertive,* and very, very *specific*.

A good thesis is like a road map.

In your thesis, don't get cute. Say exactly what you're going to prove. Give the reader a map; direct the reader to where you are going to go, what you are going to say.

Most people think that this gives away too much, that if you tell the reader too much in the beginning they will not want to read on. Wrong again!

If you are vague in the beginning, your reader will be turned off and not want to read on. On the other hand, if you set everything out in detail in the beginning, the reader will admire your specific position, even if it differs from theirs, and will want to see if you can prove it.

Consider the following two thesis sentences, again on our paper about the ozone layer:

```
Because of many reasons, we need to take further action to repair the
ozone layer.
```

```
In order to preserve the ecology, stave off the spread of cancer and
other diseases, and to save the earth, we need to force our government
to make new and stronger laws against the kinds of pollutants that are
eating away at the ozone layer.
```

The first sentence is vague, something anyone might have written. The second sentence indicates a writer who knows her stuff, someone who is in command of her topic and knows what she's talking about. This is how you want to present yourself.

✍ **Now you try it:** Write a clear, specific thesis for the paper you are working on now, on the topic you *freewrote* about on page 10.

_____
_____
_____
_____

S+T+R+O+N+G® Study Skills Program   © Silbert & Bress Publications

Step 3. Make A Detailed Outline

Step 3. Make A Detailed Outline

This is the point at which you should make one. Outlines are only hard to make if you don't have a clear, specific thesis. If you write a thesis as specific as the one above, and you name all the reasons why you think the way you do about this topic, then all you have to do is to make an outline based on what you wrote in your thesis.

Keep in mind that the thesis and the outline are meant as guidelines, not rules. You can always change them as you go along, because as you read and write your thinking about your topic might change.

Now here's an outline for the paper on the ozone layer:

Sample Outline

I. Your Introduction: (*How do I grab the reader's attention?*)
    Story about Australian children

    A. Your Thesis: (*What is my argument?*)
    In order to preserve the ecology, to stave off the spread of cancer and other diseases and to save the earth, we need to force our government to make new and stronger laws against the kind of pollutants that are eating away at the ozone layer.

II. Your Argument: (*How do I prove my thesis?*)

    A. What's happening in Australia

        1. Skin cancer

            a. article about the children

        2. Glaciers melting

    B. Events in America

        1. Rise in skin cancer

            a. story of Ellen Manuel

        2. Unusual weather patterns attributed to global warming

III. Prove Your Opponents Wrong: *(What would someone say to disagree with me? How can I shoot them down?)*

    A.   What conservative talk-show hosts have said

    B.   Critics of environmental laws

        1.   No change in weather

        2.   Too much money

        3.   Let businesses comply on their own terms

    C.   My arguments:

        1.   Proof of weather changes

        2.   Money justified in terms of quality of life

        3.   Businesses have shown they do not comply voluntarily

IV. Your Conclusion: *(So what? What should be done?)*

    A.   Pressure local congressional representatives

        1.   Letters and phone calls

        2.   Internet

    B.   Boycott products of companies that do not comply

    C.   Raise awareness

        1.   Public service addresses

        2.   Pressure news stations to show what's happening in Australia

    D.   Strong statement about the earth: the results of our disregard for the ecology because of our reverence for the economy

Step 4. Write Your Paper—Part I. Your Introduction

I. YOUR INTRODUCTION

How do I grab the reader's attention?

Once you have written your thesis and know exactly what you are going to say in your paper, or even after you've written your paper, you should think about how to start it, and how you will end it.

The two parts of a paper that give students the most trouble are the introduction and thesis. So we thought we'd talk about them first, even though you might want to write them last, after you're finished with the paper. Because sometimes as you write, you get new ideas, or change your thinking. So your introduction and thesis might change too.

Let's talk about ways to introduce your paper so that the person who reads it will want to read on.

That's one of the two main functions of your introduction: to make the reader interested, to "hook" the reader into your essay. The other is to give the reader some direction.

Your introduction has two purposes: to "hook" and direct.

Most students do neither one when they write. That's because they've never learned how. So we're going to show you how to do both! After all, if you write a good introduction, that gives the reader a good first impression. And we all know how important first impressions are.

Most students write introductions we call *general-to-specific*. They will start with a general statement on their topic and move to their more specific thesis. Consider the following introduction on our topic of school systems in Peru and America:

> Many people have lots of opinions about schools. They think their schools were OK, but are not sure what to think of other schools. But there are many different kinds of schools. Schools in Peru have lots of problems, but in some ways they are better than the schools in the United States. There are many differences between the schools, but some similarities too.

This introduction has two main problems: first, it's too general: he has written nothing that any other student couldn't have written. Second, his thesis is too general. He doesn't tell us what exactly he's going to focus on in his paper.

Sometimes *general-to-specific* introductions work well, but usually they are too general, and pretty boring. For now, try to avoid using them to start your papers.

Instead, try using one of the types of introductions described on the following pages.

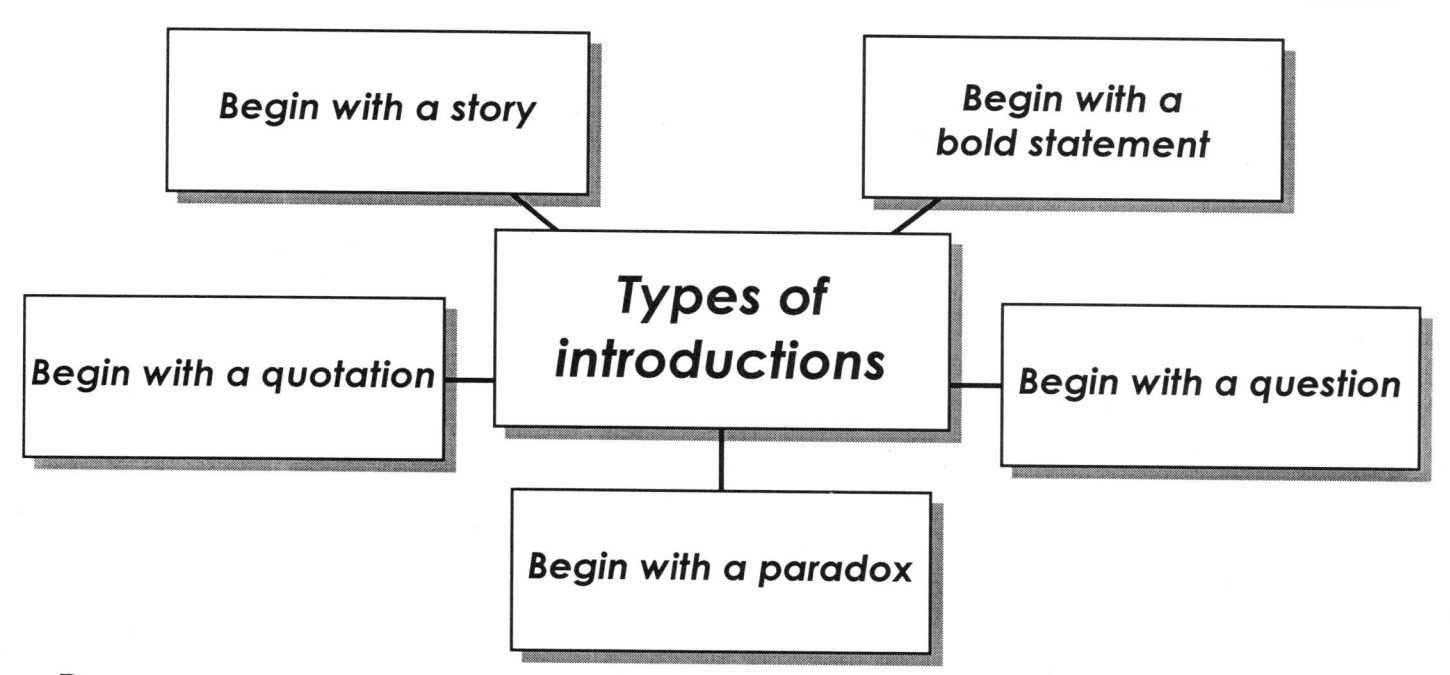

Types of introductions

- Begin with a story
- Begin with a bold statement
- Begin with a quotation
- Begin with a question
- Begin with a paradox

Remember all those times when you sat in front of your computer, or before a blank piece of paper, not knowing how to begin? Those days are over! And how about all those times you finished a paper but had no idea how to conclude it, so you just wrote, "In conclusion..." and repeated your introduction? No more! Now you'll have strategies you can use.

Begin with a story

Using this method, you would begin your paper by telling a little **story**, or anecdote, about your topic. Our paper about the ozone layer might begin like this:

On a January day in a small town in Australia, in the middle of the summer, kids are playing outside, kicking a ball around, running after each other. They look like most kids in most towns in the world, except for one thing: they are all wearing hats. And they are all wearing cakes of sun-block, level 45. And in the middle of the day, they all have to stay inside for a few hours. Why? Because most of their parents, and many of their friends, have skin cancer. Because in Australia, the hole in the ozone layer is overhead, and the glaciers are melting. And kids get skin cancer all the time.

It's not just happening in Australia. The deterioration of the ozone layer is affecting life on this planet for all of us. And it's time to do something about it. In order to preserve the ecology, to stave off the spread of cancer and other diseases, and to save the earth, we need to force the government to make new and stronger laws against the kinds of pollutants that are wearing away the ozone layer.

Beginning with a story grabs the reader's attention and directs the reader well. Now, since most people care about kids and about the state of the planet, they will read on with interest. What if the introduction had been the following? See if you can see the difference.

```
    Many people have many different opinions about the environment. Most
people don't know much about the ozone layer. It's an important part of
the environment. It affects many things about the earth, and about our
lives. Because of many reasons, we need to do take further action to
repair the ozone layer.
```

Begin with a bold statement

Another strategy is to grab the reader's attention right away with a bold, opinionated **statement**. Such openings for our two papers might be:

- "Schools in Peru are much better than schools in the United States."
- "Every day, we destroy the planet, bit by bit; and we don't seem to care much about it."

✍ *Now You Try It:* Try writing a *bold statement* to open up the paper you're working on:

_____

_____

Begin with a question

Another good way to open your paper is by asking a **question**, that your thesis, or the rest of your paper, will answer. The question could be asked right in the beginning of your paper, or it could come at the end of your introduction.

Here are possible openings for our two model topics:

- "Why are schools in poor neighborhoods in Peru better than those in the wealthy sections of the United States?"
- "What effect does the deterioration of the ozone layer have on our lives?"

✍ *Now You Try It:* Try writing a *question* to open the paper you're working on:

_____

_____

Improve Your Writing Skills

Begin with a quotation

Many students begin papers by quoting a dictionary definition of their topic: "According to Webster's Dictionary, capital punishment means..." But this is usually a big turn-off. It's boring, in other words. Why do so many students do things in their papers that are boring? Because they write with fear instead of with confidence.

But using a **quotation** to open a paper is not necessarily a bad idea. In fact, it's an attention-grabber. Just not from a dictionary, that's all. When was the last time a dictionary was exciting?

Most students write with fear instead of confidence.

So, use a quotation to open a paper, but just make sure it's

- *opinionated, or controversial;*
- *unusually well put;*
- *authoritative*
- or best of all, all three.

If you don't know much about capital punishment, for example, why not quote a famous district attorney to open your paper? Something like,

"Everyone has a right to die, but that doesn't mean we have a right to kill them."

-- Attorney I. M. Smarte

Begin with a paradox

Using this method, you begin by pointing out that while most people think one way about your topic, you will be showing that the opposite is true (**paradox**). Our model paper on school systems might use this method:

> The United States is the wealthiest nation in the world, and most visitors are amazed by the resources that are available to children in their schools: children use computers in kindergarten, teachers are paid good salaries. And when most Americans think of Peru, they think of poverty and war, and they imagine dirty kids going to school in run-down buildings. But in general, Peruvian children get a better education than American children do.

Note: By the way, you may want to return to this section when you are writing your *conclusion*. Why? Because you may use any of the above strategies to *conclude* your paper. See for yourself. Re-read each one, this time substituting the word "End" for "Begin." They work! (More about conclusions follow on page 25.)

Check Out Some Magazine Introductions: How Do They Grab You?

Find your favorite magazine and read the introductions to several articles. What kinds of introductions do these professional writers use? Do you think their introductions are effective? Do they (1) hook you into the story, and (2) give you a sense of direction about the article's main point?

Article 1

Title:

Main point of story:

Type of introduction:

Effective? Explain why or why not:

Article 2

Title:

Main point of story:

Type of introduction:

Effective? Explain why or why not:

Article 3

Title:

Main point of story:

Type of introduction:

Effective? Explain why or why not:

Improve Your Writing Skills

Step 5. Write Your Paper—Part II. Your Argument

II. YOUR ARGUMENT

How do I prove my thesis?

Once you have written your thesis, made an outline, and tried a strategy for introducing your work, then you're ready to write the body of the paper. You're ready to prove your point. It's easy to talk the talk. Now you've got to walk the walk.

There are two main types of proof: *logical* and *emotional*. Most of your paper will be spent proving your points using logic. When you do this, you appeal to your reader's reason. But depending on your topic, it might be a good idea to appeal to your reader's emotion as well. Most good persuasive papers do both.

If you don't quite understand this, think of TV and magazine advertisements. Some appeal directly to your reason: "Four out of five doctors surveyed," they might say, recommend this product. Or, this product "eliminates germs more effectively than any other mouthwash."

Others might appeal directly to your emotion: a perfume ad might depict two people in love, without mentioning anything about how the perfume smells; a beer commercial might show scenes of American landscape with music playing in the background.

And many ads try to do both: an ad for medication to get rid of pimples might explain what powerful ingredient it contains (appealing to your reason) and show how happy a teenager is at school after applying the medication (appealing to your emotion).

Assignment: Watch three TV ads. Describe their logical and/or emotional appeal.

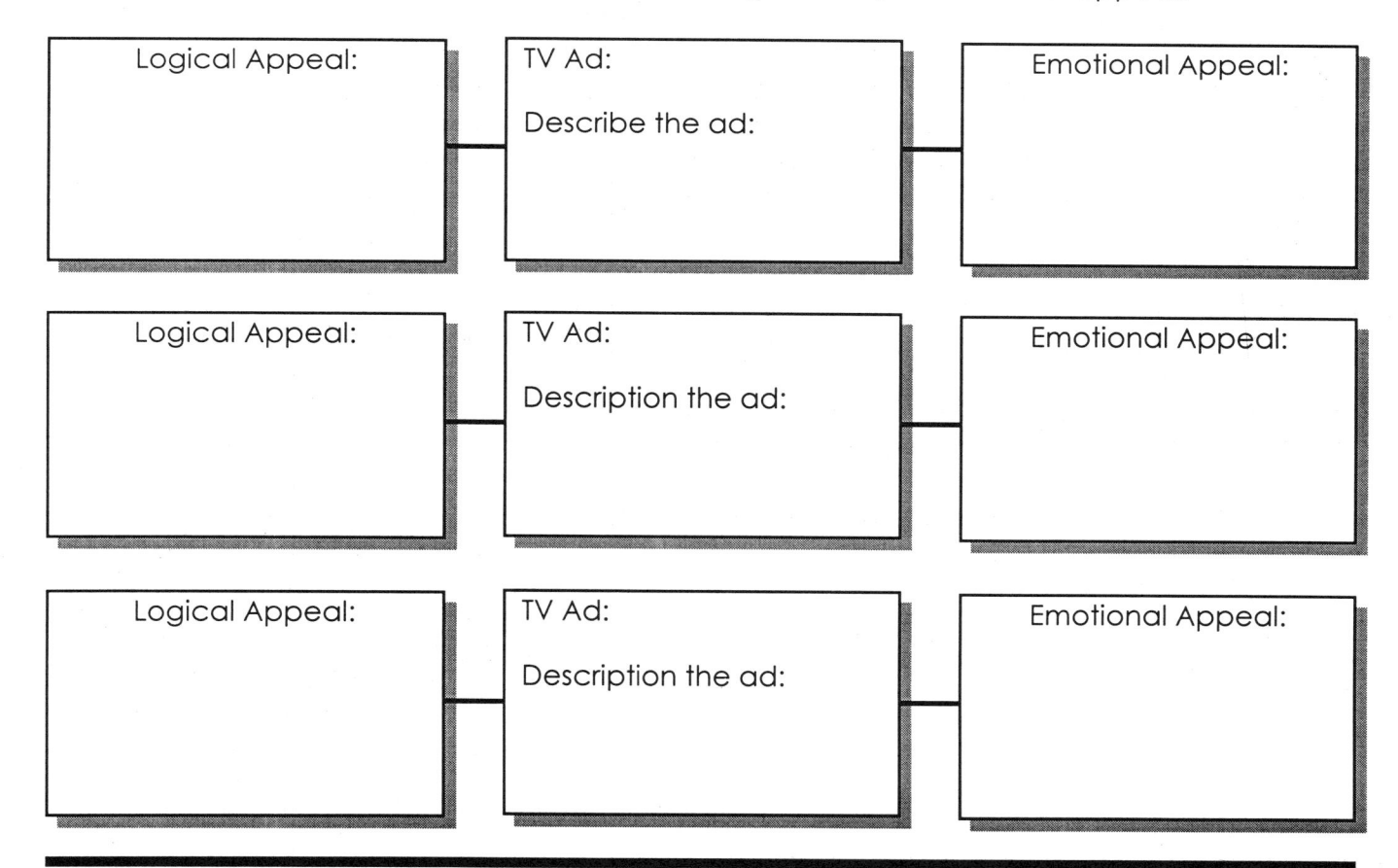

Logical Appeal:	TV Ad: Describe the ad:	Emotional Appeal:
Logical Appeal:	TV Ad: Description the ad:	Emotional Appeal:
Logical Appeal:	TV Ad: Description the ad:	Emotional Appeal:

Logical Proof:

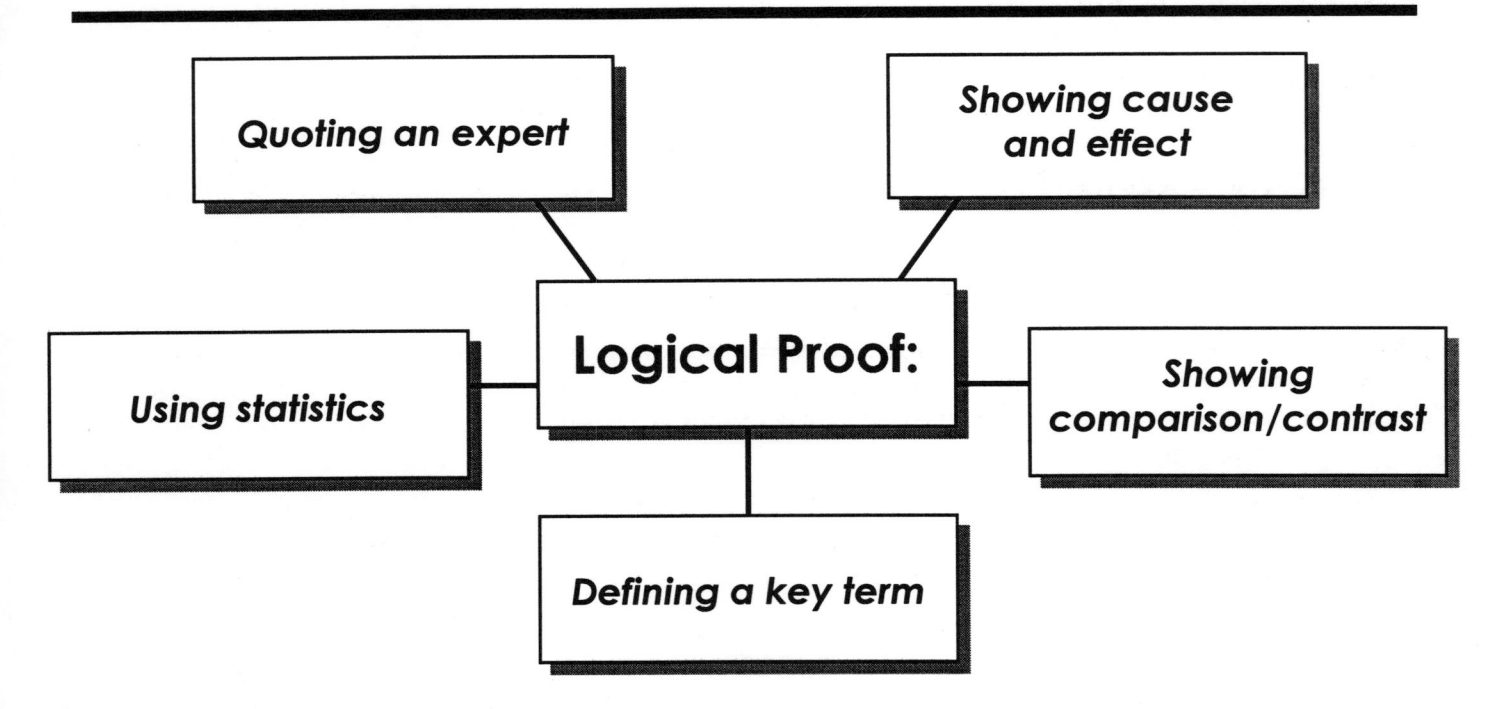

- Quoting an expert
- Showing cause and effect
- Using statistics
- Showing comparison/contrast
- Defining a key term

There are many ways to appeal to a reader's logic.

Quoting an expert

When you don't know much about your topic, don't pretend to. Research a little, and quote someone who knows more than you do about it. When you do so, you are using the "testimony" of an **expert**, just as lawyers use the testimony of experts to support the case they are trying to make.

Advertisers do this too: an actress with beautiful hair might be hired to say that she uses a certain brand of shampoo, or a famous basketball player will say that he wears a certain brand of sneaker. If companies just told you how good the shampoo or sneaker was, you would not be likely to buy it. But since an "expert" endorses it, you might.

Similarly, when you are trying to prove your point, quoting or paraphrasing an expert will help you to do so. Our environment paper might quote a well-known environmentalist, an Australian who has felt the effects of the ozone hole, or a writer who has written an opinionated essay on the topic. Our school-system paper might quote a Peruvian schoolchild or someone who wrote an article on the topic in an education journal.

"Will that be cash or charge?"

Improve Your Writing Skills

🖎 **Now You Try It:** Find an expert on any subject and quote what he or she has to say about it. You could ask a member of the basketball team a question on free-throw shooting, or ask a history teacher about the Civil War.

Question:_____

_____

Answer: _____

_____

_____

_____

_____

_____

| *Showing cause and effect* | Write about what will be the effect of certain events, what will result if something happens. You can discuss the effects of the current situation if allowed to stand, or the effects of the kinds of suggestions you are proposing. |

In our ozone paper, for example, we could spend a good deal of time explaining what would be the effects of allowing that hole to widen, or what would happen (the **effect**) if the government took action against pollutants that damage it (the **cause**).

Advertisers use this technique as well. For example, one medicine company might tell you that if you use their product regularly (the *cause*), then your illness will go away (the *effect*).

| *Using statistics* | It always helps to have numbers to back you up: commercials do this all the time when they tell you that a cereal contains 100% of the recommended daily amount of most major vitamins, or that seven out of every ten people surveyed preferred this cola over the other. |

In our school-system paper we could help prove our point by using **statistics**. We could find in one article, for example, that 85% of all Americans have a poor opinion of their school while only 43% of Peruvians do, or that American schools have 90% more resources than schools in Peru. In our environment paper we could mention that the Antarctic glaciers have melted by more than ¼ of their size of 20 years ago.

Helpful hint: Be careful not to overuse statistics. Too many statistics in a row and your reader will be asleep in no time.

| *Defining a key term* | You appeal to your reader's logic also when you **define** an important term that you're using. Do this not by providing a dictionary definition, but by explaining how you will be using this term. You could, for example, write a few sentences explaining what you mean when you use the term *acid rain*. |

Showing comparison/contrast

Comparison is an explanation of the similarities between two or more things; **Contrast** is an explanation of the differences. You appeal to your reader's reason when you compare and contrast different elements of your topic.

You could compare and contrast something in one paragraph, or over the course of a paper. To do so, use the A/B format. To explain this format let's take our paper on schools as an example:

Examples: School Systems (A = schools in Peru, B = schools in the United States)

```
Teaching behaviors
     A.
     B.
Resources
     A.
     B.
Student performances on tests
     A.
     B.
```

Or, you could use a different approach:

```
A (Peru):   Teaching behaviors
            Resources
            Student performances on tests
B (U.S.):   Teaching behaviors
            Resources
            Student performances on tests
```

There are many other ways to appeal to the reader's logic, like using facts, explaining how something works, and giving the background or history of a subject. But again, the best way to prove something is by using examples. When you show your reader that you're not just saying something is true, but that there is evidence that it is true, your reader will believe you. When you just say so, without anything to back it up, the reader will not be convinced.

Improve Your Writing Skills

Emotional Proof

- *A moving story*
- *A passionate tone*

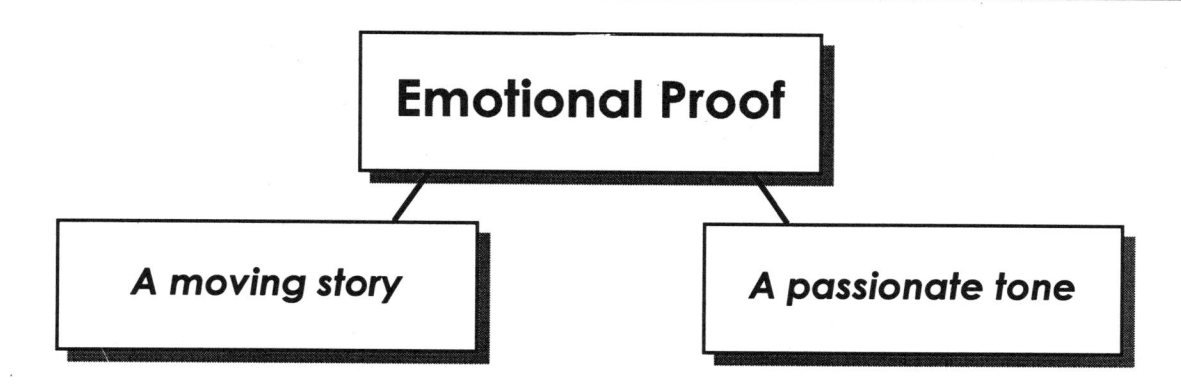

It is most important to convince your reader to believe you by using your reason, as we just illustrated. But appealing to the reader's **emotions** is important too. To do so, you can include **a moving story** or a **passionate tone**.

In our paper on the ozone layer we could do both. We could include at the end of the paper (emotional appeals are usually best toward the end) a paragraph like this one:

> Amy Jennings used to be a lively, pretty seven-year-old who loved to play on the new swing set she got for Christmas last year. Now, after having her face, arms and legs burned to a crisp one hot Saturday afternoon, she spends her days confined indoors, often staring out the window. Her life has been ruined by skin cancer. How many other lives must be ruined before we take action? How much more evidence do we have to see before we start fixing this problem?

Emotional appeals, whether by story or tone, are often very effective. Sometimes in order to get a bill passed Congressional representatives and Senators will ask people who have gone through traumatic experiences to speak before Congress. Late-night television ads for charities that help children will just show pictures of beautiful, starving children. They know that the most effective way to get people to write them a check is to appeal to their emotions (they also appeal to your logic, by telling you, for example, that the amount it takes to help a child is the same as a pack of gum every day—that's using *comparison/contrast*).

✎ **Now you try it:** Add an emotional appeal to the end of the paper you're writing:

_____
_____
_____
_____
_____
_____
_____
_____

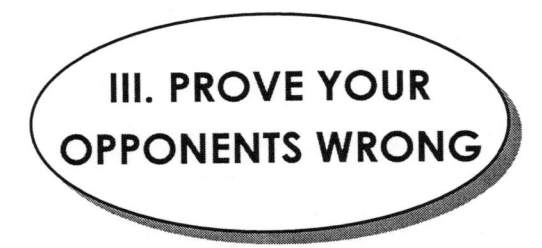

Step 6. Write Your Paper—Part III. Prove Your Opponents Wrong

III. PROVE YOUR OPPONENTS WRONG

How can I shoot down my opponents' arguments?

Once you have proven your thesis, by using reason and emotion, you should think about what someone who disagrees with you might say. If you then prove this other way of thinking wrong, you have *refuted* them, and your paper will be more convincing.

Let's say you support capital punishment: you think people who commit murder should be put to death. You could make a very compelling argument for your case, mentioning examples of murderers who have gotten out of prison to commit more crimes, and telling the story of someone who was killed to appeal to the reader's emotion.

But you also need to think about the person who believes capital punishment is wrong. If you ignore what that person would say against capital punishment then the only people you will convince are those who already agree with you to begin with.

So, you should think of what they would say, and *refute* their arguments (prove them wrong), again by using logic and emotion. You might bring up the fact that some states have life imprisonment without parole, or that capital punishment costs taxpayers more than putting a criminal in prison, or that some people think it is morally wrong. Then if you refute these claims you may convince the reader who would normally disagree with you. You might, for example, use reason by saying that it only costs more because of the appeal processes, which you would propose limiting.

Toward the end of our paper on school systems, we might write something like this.

> Some people might think that teachers in Peru are too strict, that they discipline their students too harshly. But they have strict rules against physical punishment, and the academic results are amazing. So maybe American teachers aren't strict enough!

"What's there to argue? Anyone who disagrees with me is WRONG!"

24   *Improve Your Writing Skills*

Step 7. Write Your Paper—Part IV. Your Conclusion

IV. YOUR CONCLUSION

So what? What should be done?

Conclusions should answer the question, So what? You have spent many paragraphs discussing a problem, writing in detail about some subject. Now, when it comes time to end, ask yourself, So? So now what? So what needs to be done? If you answer these questions you've got yourself a new conclusion.

At the end of our paper on the ozone layer, for example, we might ask ourselves, So what? The result might be something like this:

> We need to enforce laws which prohibit harmful fluorocarbons that harm the quality of our air and eat away at the ozone layer. If there is enough public pressure to enforce such laws then companies will not do further damage. In fact as some experts say we can even repair it.

So often students almost complete their papers, and then sit there, not knowing how to finish. So they end up just repeating their introduction. Again: this is BORING! And anyway, your paper isn't all that long. The reader still remembers what you wrote in your first paragraph.

Instead, try to use one of the techniques listed under Introductions (page 15), this time using them to end your paper.

Types of Conclusions:

- End with a story
- End with a bold statement
- End with a question
- End with a quotation
- End with a paradox

Here are two possible endings to our school-system paper. The first ends with a bold statement, the second with a question:

> - Schools in Peru are simply better than those in the United States.
> - Considering all the evidence, wouldn't it be smarter for the United States government to spend a few billion dollars more on teacher training, and a few billion less on playground equipment?

Put It All Together—Your Paper

"I must be delirious—
I think I've got it!
Here goes..."

All along, we have been asking you to write about one of the topics listed on page 10. But, if you want to pick your own topic for a paper, that's great. Pick something that interests you, not something you think you should write about. Instead of writing about a general or typical topic like abortion or capital punishment, write about something you are interested in, whether it's hiking or car engines.

We have shown you how to make a persuasive argument. Now you can do it yourself!

Now You Try It: Follow the guideline to a persuasive paper, below, and begin to construct this paper. Feel free to use what you wrote in previous exercises in this book.

I. Your Introduction: _____
_____
_____
_____

A. Your Thesis: _____
_____

II. Your Argument

A. Logical Proof: (quoting someone else, showing cause and effect, using statistics, defining a key term, comparison/contrast)

_____
_____
_____
_____
_____
_____
_____
_____
_____

26 *Improve Your Writing Skills*

B. Emotional Proof: (A moving story and/or a passionate tone)

_____
_____
_____
_____
_____

III. Prove Your Opponents Wrong: (What would your opponents say? How can you prove their arguments wrong? _____
_____
_____
_____
_____
_____
_____
_____
_____
_____
_____
_____

IV. Your Conclusion: (So what? What should be done?)_____
_____
_____
_____
_____
_____

> Keep in mind, you don't have to follow this kind of outline. This is just meant to give you an idea of how you might organize your thinking when you write a paper, and how to be as convincing as possible. (For example, many good writers save their emotional appeal for the very end.)

Step 8. Revise and Edit Your Paper

"Hey, what's this with revising? I thought I was done!"

Revising means re-seeing. This is when you reshape and bring into focus what you really what to say, and see if you have said it effectively.

Do you want to know why most students get C's, D's and F's on their papers? It's usually not because they're dumb. It's usually because they write their papers at the last minute, and once the last word is typed or written, they put it away and hand it in without changing a thing.

Dumb idea. Most papers will improve by a whole grade if you simply take time to revise them: this means reading your papers over and checking to see if the words you use, and the way the paper is organized and written, get across exactly what you're trying to say. So, Mr. or Ms. Editor, let's edit.

✏️✏️✏️ Revising and Editing Checklist ✏️✏️✏️

Here's a **checklist** for you to follow when it comes time to revise and edit your paper:

☐ **Did I leave enough time?** Pretty obvious, but it's amazing how we put off our homework until the last minute, isn't it? Well, if there's one subject you shouldn't do this with, it's writing. If you have a paper due on Friday, then do it on Tuesday, revise it on Wednesday, and proofread it on Thursday. Then watch your grades go up, up, up!

☐ **Did I get some help?** Got any friends? Then use them. Read your paper out loud to them and tell them you want some advice on how to improve it. Better yet, do your paper a couple of days early and ask your teacher to look it over. She or he will probably be happy to do so, and then when it comes time to grade your paper, will remember that you have been working on it more than the other students have.

☐ **Did I check for transitions?** Look at the beginning of each paragraph. Have you provided a "bridge" from the paragraph preceding it? If not, build one! How? Circle a transitional word or phrase (see page 6 for a list of transitional phrases) when you see one, and add one if you don't. This will help make your paper more "connected."

☐ **Do I have a good title?** The titles of movies and books sometimes have a lot to do with their success. Even though the best title in the world can't turn a poorly written paper into a superior one, it will help your paper to have a clever or appropriate title. So don't just type "Paper 1." Think of a good title that will *help* its appeal, not hurt it.

☐ **Do I have a good thesis?** What is my main idea, or my thesis? Do I make it clear soon enough and keep my focus throughout my paper? Check to see if you followed through on what you promised in your thesis. Did you prove what you promised you would prove, or did you lose your focus somewhere along the way? If you don't end up proving what you say you will prove, then change the thesis or change the body of your paper so that you stay consistent throughout.

- **Do I develop my thesis and main points enough?** Are my general statements and ideas supported by appropriate concrete details and examples? You develop your ideas through illustration, through examples. Do you make general statements only to move onto the next idea? Stop and add an example, so you're showing, not just telling.

- **Is each paragraph unified by a topic sentence or topic idea?** Just as every well-organized paper has a clear and specific thesis, most good paragraphs have clear and specific topic sentences. Check to see if yours do.

- **Is my organization reasonable?** Does each point lead to the next? Do you have a plan? Are there parts of this paper that have nothing to do with your focus?

- **Is my introduction interesting and focused?**

- **Is my conclusion interesting and not repetitive?**

- **How is my tone?** Is your tone formal enough? Not too formal? Are you too careful, sarcastic, or apologetic?

- **Did I cut out words and phrases that don't mean anything**, like "basically," "really," "very," "in my opinion," "personally," and so on?

- *Do I have any run-ons?* If you have any sentences with more than one *independent clause* (an *independent clause* is one that can stand on its own as a sentence), and the clauses are separated by only a comma, it is probably a run-on (or *fused sentence*). Fix it by using a semicolon, or comma and helping word. Look at this example:

    (original)   Sports are great, they help keep kids off the streets.
    (corrected)   Sports are great; they help keep kids off the streets.
    (corrected)   Sports are great, because they help keep kids off the street.

- **Do I have any fragments?** If you have a sentence that is a *dependent clause* (it depends upon another clause to make a complete sentence), it is a *fragment*. Fix it by making it into, or combining it with, an *independent clause*.

- **Have I read the paper out loud?** Sometimes, by hearing yourself read the words out loud, you can catch mistakes you may have missed.

- **Do nouns and verbs agree in every sentence? If the noun is plural, is the verb plural?** Also, be careful not to start a paragraph in the present tense and finish it in the past tense. This is especially common when students write about literature, which they should do in the present, not past, tense. For example, write

    "Holden Caufield is brave when he stands up to his friends" instead of
    "Holden Caufield was brave when he stood up to his friends."

    Check to make sure your nouns agree with your verbs. That means if you use the noun "Both men" the verb should be plural, or if you use "Each man" then the verb should be singular.

    For example, "Both men lose their lives in the battle;" "Each man loses his life in the battle."

☐ **Do I use the same subject throughout each paragraph?** If you start by saying "People" or "Everyone" do you switch to "you" or "I" or "one"? Are you consistent?

Be extra careful about this one. So many students make this mistake! Look at each paragraph. Notice what subject you use. If you write, "Everyone thinks that schools in Peru are run-down," the next sentences should not be, "But one needs to avoid such stereotypes. People should keep their minds open." Your subject is everyone, one, then people. Stick with one throughout the paragraph and don't jump around.

☐ **Have I checked for spelling errors?**

☐ **Is my style interesting or monotonous?** Are my sentences of varying length, or are they all the same length? Are there some short sentences, some long? Can some of my short sentences be combined?

Check the length of your sentences. Chances are, many of them are about the same length and are constructed in the same way. There are two things you should do: First, combine some short sentences to make an occasional complex sentence. Second, change some sentences so that they do not all have the same subject-verb-object construction.

As an example, consider the following sentences:

> I never used to think about the ozone layer. I knew nothing about global warming. I didn't care too much about the environment in general. But I think about it all the time now.

Now, since these sentences are monotonous, let's combine two and switch the construction of another:

> I never used to think about the ozone layer, and about global warming I knew nothing. I didn't care too much about the environment in general. But now, I think about it all the time.

☐ **Have I chosen my words carefully?** Do the words I've used reflect what I really want to say, or are they common words that don't say exactly what I mean? Are you talking around your point, instead of making it directly and succinctly?

☐ **Do I use the active voice instead of the passive?** Always try to use the active voice. Look at this example:

> (passive) When sports are played, more self-confidence results.
> (active) When kids play sports, they become more confident.

Note: It may seem like a lot of work to ask yourself all these questions, but ask yourself, don't you want to get B's and A's instead of D's? Don't you want to learn how to communicate better, since clear communication will help you in almost every area of your life (including your job and your relationships)?

"Editing? Thanks anyway, but I'll pass."

Your Finished Paper

In the space below or on a computer word processor, write a revised and edited version of the paper you've been working on throughout this workbook. Use additional pages as needed. By the way, congratulations, you made it!